The Lord's Prayer

Illustrated by Lara Ede

make
believe
ideas

Our Father in heaven, hallowed be Your name.

Your **kingdom** come,

Your **Will** be **done,** on **earth** as in **heaven.**

Give us today our **daily bread.**

Forgive us our sins,

as we **forgive** those who sin against **us.**

Lead us not into **temptation,**

but **deliver** us from evil.

For the **kingdom**,
the **power**,
and the **glory** are Yours.

Now and **forever.** Amen.